History and Invention

The Wheel and How It Changed the World

The Clock and How It Changed the World

The Light Bulb and How It Changed the World

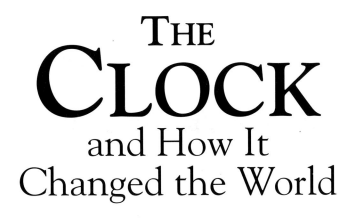

THE
CLOCK
and How It
Changed the World

THE
CLOCK
and How It
Changed the World

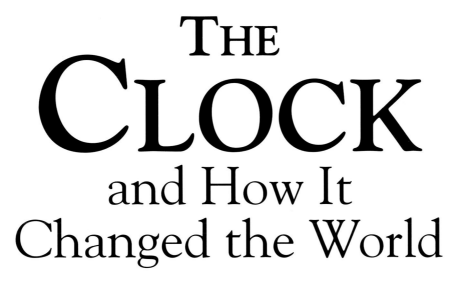

Michael Pollard

Facts On File®

AN INFOBASE HOLDINGS COMPANY

Facts On File, Inc.
460 Park Avenue South
New York NY 10016

First published in the United States by Facts On File, Inc. in 1995.
First published in the United Kingdom by Simon & Schuster Young Books.

Library of Congress Cataloging-in-Publication Data
Pollard, Michael, 1931–
    The clock and how it changed the world / Michael Pollard.
        p.   cm.   — (History and invention)
    Includes bibliographical references and index.
    ISBN 0-8160-3142-8
    1. Clocks and watches—Juvenile literature.   2. Time—Juvenile
literature.   [1. Clocks and watches—History.   2. Time.
3. Inventions.]   I. Title.   II. Series
TS542.5.P65   1995
681.1'13—dc20
                                                94–15225

A CIP catalogue record for this book is available from the British Library

Facts On File books are available at special discounts when purchased in bulk quantities for businesses, associations, institutions or sales promotions. Please call our Special Sales Department in New York at 212/683-2244 or 800/322-8755.

10 9 8 7 6 5 4 3 2 1

Printed and bound in Hong Kong

Picture Acknowledgments:

The publisher would like to thank the following sources for permission to use copyright material:
BT Pictures: p 37 below; Barnaby's Picture Library: contents page left; Bridgeman Art Library: pp 10, 13 top and bottom, 18, 19; Christies Colour Library: title page, copyright page top; Mary Evans Picture Library: pp 22-23, 23 top, 25 top, 26 top, 27 top, 31 bottom, 43 left; Robert Harding Picture Library: pp 8 left and bottom, 35 bottom, 39; Michael Holford: pp copyright page bottom, contents page right, 11, 14, 15 all, 16, 17, 25 bottom, 26 bottom, 27 above center, center, bottom, 28 center all, 29; Hulton Picture Company: pp 30 below, 36; The Mansell Collection Limited: pp 20, 21 below, 24; Peter Newark/Western Americana: p 42; Popperfoto: pp 33 top, 38 left; Tony Stone Worldwide: pp 37 top, 38 right; Zefa Picture Library: pp 8 right, 9, 28 below, 31 top, 33 bottom, 41, 43 right.

CONTENTS

EVERYDAY USES OF TIME

When do you get up in the morning? What time does the bus leave? When shall we have dinner? How long will it take to cook the pie? When does your favorite television show start? Our lives revolve around time. We go to work, school or leisure activities at fixed times. Buses, trains and airplanes run to timetables. Shops and offices have times for opening and closing. Whenever we go on a trip we calculate how much time it will take. Our ability to measure time brings order into our lives and helps us to plan ahead.

"Rush hours" are a feature of city life, when people travel to and from work. This rush hour crowd is in the Chinese city of Lanzhou.

In athletics, a fraction of a second may make the difference between winning or losing a medal.

Time and speed

There would be no way of measuring speed if we could not tell the time. Speed is calculated as the distance traveled by an object in a certain period of time. For many calculations, such as measuring how fast a car is traveling, it is sufficient to work out the speed in miles per hour. Sometimes, however, we need to work out speeds by the distance traveled in a second, or even in a fraction of a second.

A precision stopwatch used to time competing athletes' performances to fractions of a second.

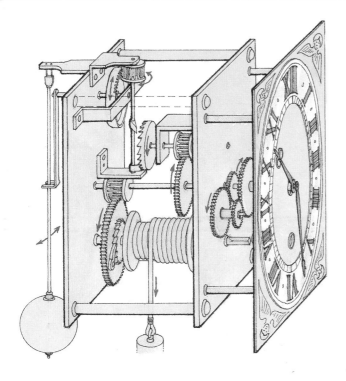

Mechanical clocks

The first mechanical clocks were made in Europe in the mid-13th century. The mechanism was a drum with a rope wound around it. A heavy weight was fixed to the free end of the rope. As the weight dropped, the rope unwound, the drum turned and a hand moved around the clock face.

The mainspring was invented about 200 years later. This device stored energy, which it released slowly as it unwound. Heavy weights were no longer needed.

The next important invention came in 1657 when Christian Huygens, a Dutch astronomer, made the first pendulum clock. A pendulum is a rod with a weight at the end. The time the pendulum takes to make one complete swing depends on the length of the rod, but each swing takes the same time. This more accurate way of telling the time helped him with his observations of the night sky.

Christian Huygens' pendulum clock provided a new standard of accuracy. It was the first to record minutes as well as hours.

Air traffic controllers on duty in the control tower of a busy airport. Air safety depends on precise timekeeping to separate aircraft taking off, landing and in flight.

The search for accuracy

Huygens' pendulum clock kept time more accurately than any clock that had been made before, but it would be of little use to us today. We expect clocks to measure short periods of time with the greatest accuracy and to stay accurate for months or even years without being corrected.

Many aspects of modern life depend on split-second timing. The navigation of ships through crowded waterways and the control of air traffic around busy airports are two examples. Nowadays the clocks that time these operations are driven electronically. They are accurate to within thousandths of a second.

THE BEGINNINGS OF TIME AND CLOCKS

Until about 200 years ago, most people in the world worked on the land. They farmed and raised livestock just like the people of the ancient world. People's lives were ruled by the sun. They started work at sunrise. In the middle of the day they paused to eat, when the sun was highest. When the sun set, they stopped work and went home. People had no need for clocks or watches. Church bells or calls from the mosque told them when it was time for worship and prayer.

Counting the hours

The year, the month and the day are periods of time that are fixed by the movement of the Earth and its moon. Smaller units of time were devised by humans. These are the hour, the minute and the second.

There is no real reason why there should be 24 hours in a day, or 60 minutes in an hour, or 60 seconds in a minute. These were the divisions of time chosen by the ancient civilizations of the Middle East that people have used ever since.

Candles and sandglasses

Water clocks and sundials were only rough guides to time. There were many attempts to find more precise methods of timekeeping before the invention of the mechanical clock. One device was the candle clock. This was simply a large candle with the hours marked down its

Even until recent times, farming societies had little need of clocks. Their activities were determined by the seasons and the length of the day.

These were some of the timekeeping devices used before the invention of mechanical clocks. From left to right: the sandglass or hourglass, the water clock, the sundial and the Chinese fire clock.

Except for the sundial, these did not give a continuous reading but were useful for measuring periods of time.

length. The hours were marked out as the candle burned down. The sandglass or hourglass was a device which was used at sea. The sand in the top half of the glass took a fixed time to trickle through to the bottom half. Usually this was half an hour or an hour. Someone had to stand by the timer to turn the glass upside-down at the end of the period. This was the job of one of the boys in the crew.

Candle clocks and sandglasses measured only *periods* of time. They did not show the hour of the day. Both had an advantage over the sundial, however. They could be used at night and on cloudy days.

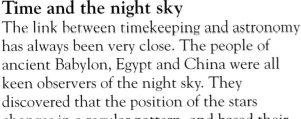

Time and the night sky

The link between timekeeping and astronomy has always been very close. The people of ancient Babylon, Egypt and China were all keen observers of the night sky. They discovered that the position of the stars changes in a regular pattern, and based their divisions of time on these changes. More recent inventors of clocks have also been interested in astronomy, including Pope Sylvester II and Christian Huygens. The link between time and the stars soon meant that people needed more accurate types of clock – especially for sailing.

The Tower of the Winds was a public clock in the center of Athens. It consisted of a water clock and a sundial.

Cathedral clocks

One of the first uses of mechanical clocks was to let people know when it was time to go to church. There is a story that the first clock was invented by Pope Sylvester II in about the year 1000. Clocks were seen in many European cathedrals by about 1300. As well as keeping time, some clock faces showed the phases of the moon and gave other astronomical information. Many of these clocks had bells that rang to call people to worship. The oldest mechanical clock still working is in Salisbury Cathedral in England. It was built in 1386.

The invention of the mainspring made it possible to build small clocks for the homes of wealthy people. Germany was the center of a busy clockmaking industry by 1600. Clocks were made individually, often as much for decoration as for telling the time. They became prized possessions that the owners could show off to their friends.

Part of the mechanism of the 600-year-old clock in Salisbury Cathedral, England. The clock is of the rope-and-drum type.

The shadow clock was a form of sundial.

Although the early mechanical clocks measured time better than candles or sandglasses, they were not very accurate. They had to be checked frequently against sundials or by astronomical observations. Sailors were most affected by the lack of accurate timekeeping. Ancient Egyptian sailors found their way by staying within sight of land and using landmarks to work out their position. Once sailors became more adventurous they needed a means of navigation across open sea. This depended on being able to calculate their position at any time of day or night.

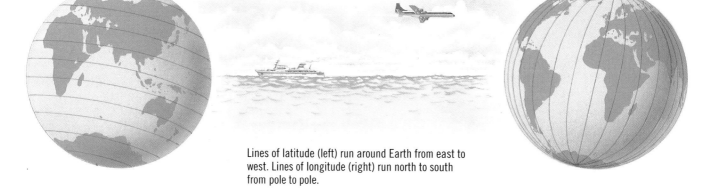

Lines of latitude (left) run around Earth from east to west. Lines of longitude (right) run north to south from pole to pole.

Aids to navigation

Navigation depends on knowing your position on Earth's surface and the position of your destination. You can then work out the direction, or course, to sail. But winds or tides may carry your ship off course, so regular checks are needed.

The earliest aids to navigation were the stars. The ancient Greeks invented an instrument, the astrolabe, to work out their ships' locations. Calculations were possible only at night when the skies were clear. By the early 1100s, the magnetic compass had come into use. This enabled ships to steer a fairly accurate course in fine weather. In rough seas it was not easy to keep these first compasses steady enough to give an accurate reading.

The next development was the sextant. Invented in 1731, this was an optical instrument that measured the height of the sun. Taking this measurement at noon, when the sun was at its highest, a sailor could work out the ship's latitude. All these instruments made sailors' lives easier and safer, but they left one problem still unsolved. This was how to work out the ship's longitude accurately. Without this, estimates of the ship's position along a line of latitude were not much more than guesswork.

The sextant enables the angle of the sun at noon to be measured. An image of the sun is superimposed on an image of the horizon, and the angle between the two is marked on a scale. Latitude can be calculated from this angle.

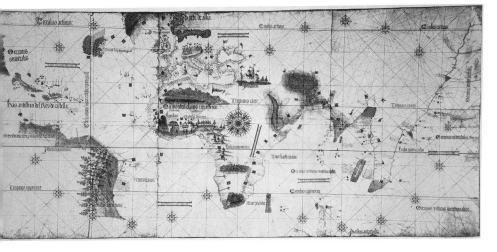

Published in 1502, this world map gives a surprisingly accurate picture of Europe, the Mediterranean, Africa and the coast of southeast Asia.

Dead reckoning

The best method for sailors to estimate their position was a system called "dead reckoning." Using a compass, the navigator plotted the course that the ship was to take. The next step was to calculate the ship's speed along the course by "log and line." A log was tied to the end of a long rope in which knots had been tied at intervals. The log was thrown overboard and a sandglass was turned over. When the top of the sandglass was empty, sailors hauled in the rope and counted the knots. In this way the navigator would work out how far the ship had sailed along its course. The speed at which ships travel is still measured in knots.

Dangerous waters

It is surprising to think that the great European explorations of the 15th and 16th centuries were made using only the astrolabe, the compass and dead reckoning. Explorers like Christopher Columbus and Ferdinand Magellan were not heading for any particular destination, however. When their discoveries led to trade between Europe and the newly found continents the problem of navigation became acute.

No one could tell how long a voyage would last or how much food to take for the crew. Cargoes of fresh fruit and vegetables often rotted before the ships reached port. Many ships simply disappeared, victims of storms or poor navigation that ran them aground on rocks. Answers needed to be found for the problems of elusive longitude measurement and inaccurate time keeping.

Dead reckoning was the best means of navigation that sailors had for centuries, but winds and tidal movements made it hopelessly inaccurate.

Standardizing Longitude and Time

Everywhere in the world, the sun reaches its highest point in the sky at 12 o'clock noon. Since Earth rotates around its axis once each day, noon does not come everywhere at the same time. If it is noon where you live, it is also noon only in places that are along the same meridian, or line of longitude.

Memphis, Tennessee, is at longitude 90 degrees west. When it is noon in Memphis it is also noon in New Orleans, on the same line of longitude to the south, and at Thunder Bay in Canada to the north. For all these places it is noon "local time."

The original Royal Observatory at Greenwich, London. It was founded in 1675 to collect and publish astronomical information to help navigators and to provide a standard for the measurement of longitude – the Greenwich or Prime Meridian.

The Prime Meridian

The calculation of longitude depends on knowing the time in two places and working out the difference between the readings. "Standard time" is the time at a place whose longitude is known. "Local time" is the time at the position of a ship when the calculation is made.

Before time checks could be received by radio, a ship needed a clock set to standard time that would stay accurate throughout the voyage. In the 17th century, Britain was the world's leading seafaring nation. In 1675, the British decided to take "standard time" as the time at the Royal Observatory at Greenwich in southeast London. The line of longitude passing through Greenwich became 0 degrees. Other lines of longitude were measured as east or west of Greenwich. Some other countries chose different places to mark 0 degrees. This did not matter until ships were able to communicate with each other by radio. Finally the Greenwich system became international in 1884.

The challenge

By the beginning of the 18th century, sailors knew that a reliable clock on board was the key to accurate navigation. The problem was that the clock would have to be able to stand up to conditions at sea. Pendulum clocks were useless because the swing of the pendulum was upset by the motion of the ship. The spring clocks that had been built so far needed regular checking against other clocks or against the sun. What was needed was a clock that would keep going and show the correct "standard time" for weeks on end, even under the challenging conditions of an ocean voyage.

Storms remain a threat to sailors, as they always have been. Apart from the danger of shipwreck, in the past there was also the possibility of being blown off course.

Three stages in the history of timekeeping. *Top*, an 11th-century Chinese water clock mechanism. *Middle*, the astrological clock in St. Mark's Square, Venice, with a 24-hour clock-face. *Bottom*, an English sandglass made at the end of the 16th century.

At the beginning of the 18th century, there was a great power struggle in Europe. The two contestants were Britain and France. Both countries were trying to build up empires in North America, the West Indies and India. They looked forward to the wealth that trade with their empires would bring them. The arena for this conflict was the Atlantic Ocean. Britain and France both needed trade across the Atlantic and so built huge navies to protect their merchant ships and defend their

The chronometer competition

The British government became so alarmed by the loss of naval and merchant ships in the Atlantic that, in 1714, it announced a competition for the design of an accurate ship's chronometer. The prize was to be £20,000 – a fortune in those days (in 1994, $30,000).

The rules of the competition were strict. The British government wanted a chronometer that would give a longitude reading accurate to within 30 nautical miles (about 55 kilometers) after six weeks at sea. This meant that the chronometers must neither gain nor lose more than three seconds a day.

At that time this was a huge technical challenge since no clock had achieved such accuracy, even on dry land. The winning chronometer had to be the most accurate clock ever invented to cope with the rolling of the ship, the salty sea air and changes in temperature and humidity.

The winner

John Harrison was a clockmaker from Yorkshire who was only 20 when the competition was announced. He devoted most of his life to perfecting the winning chronometer. In 1759, after three earlier failed attempts, he succeeded.

Two years later, Harrison's son William took the chronometer on a six-week voyage from Britain to Jamaica. On its return it was found to have lost an average of only 2.7 seconds per day. It could give a longitude reading accurate to within 30 kilometers (about 16 nautical miles). The story has a sour ending. It took John Harrison 12 years to persuade the government to hand over his prize.

Copies of John Harrison's chronometer were made for the British Navy by a London watchmaker, Larcum Kendall. This one, made in 1774, was used by Captain Cook on his third and final voyage to the southern Pacific on board HMS *Discovery*.

possessions. But the Atlantic is a hazardous ocean. In spring and autumn, south-westerly winds whip up the sea into enormous waves, which either sent the small ships of the time wildly off course or caused them to sink. In spring and summer, the Arctic released icebergs that floated south down the eastern coast of North America, crushing any ships in their path. Apart from these hazards, it was hard to maintain a course across over 32,000,000 square miles (82,000,000 sq. km.) of ocean.

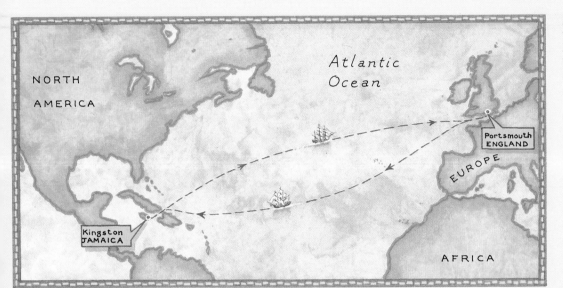

A voyage to the West Indies across the hazardous and unpredictable Atlantic was one of the severest tests that could have been devised for John Harrison's chronometer.

The French rival

Rivalry between Britain and France extended to the invention of the most accurate chronometer. John Harrison only just won the race. In 1765, a Paris clockmaker called Pierre Le Roy made a chronometer that was almost as accurate. As so often with new inventions, several people at the forefront of technology were working independently on similar ideas at the same time. Clocks had solved the problems of navigation and the seas would now become great and busy highways.

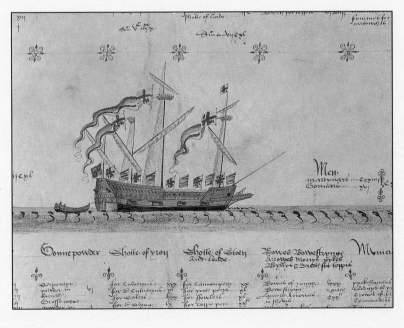

HMS *Unicorn* was part of Henry VIII's battle fleet. This contemporary picture also shows part of the ship's inventory listing its armaments.

The invention of chronometers did not change life at sea overnight. For one thing chronometers were expensive. Clockmakers in Britain and France spent many years trying to copy John Harrison's and Pierre Le Roy's prototypes more cheaply. It wasn't until 1800 that chronometers came into general use. With the sextant, they made navigation at sea more certain. In 1702, Britain had 3,300 merchant ships, but by 1800 there were almost 17,500. Other European countries such as France and the Netherlands had smaller merchant fleets that also grew rapidly during the 18th century. The great ports included London, Bordeaux, Amsterdam, Hamburg and Boston, Massachusetts. These expanded by taking in more land for docks, quays and storage space so that they could load and unload cargo more quickly and efficiently.

The merchant routes

The new aids to navigation made it possible for ships' masters to plot their courses accurately, and they soon built up a network of routes that gave the fastest and safest voyages. The number of losses at sea fell. In both Europe and North America, lighthouses were built to warn ships of dangerous rocks and headlands. Wood or coal fires were lit at the top of beacon towers at first. Later, these fires were replaced by lamps.

As voyages became less risky, people made fortunes by investing in ships and their cargo.

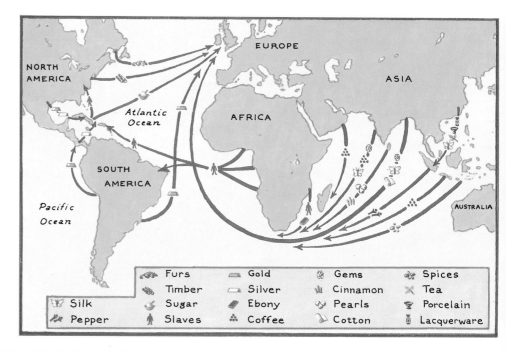

	Furs		Gold		Gems		Spices
	Timber		Silver		Cinnamon		Tea
	Silk		Sugar		Ebony		Pearls		Porcelain
	Pepper		Slaves		Coffee		Cotton		Lacquerware

The fortified port of Valletta on the Mediterranean island of Malta. Britain acquired Malta in 1814 after the war with France, and made Valletta a key port for Mediterranean trade.

As the network of world shipping routes grew, ports were built on nearby coasts, and on islands en route, to renew ships' supplies of food and water. Later, when steamships were introduced, these ports also enabled ships to restock with coal.

The Battle of Trafalgar in 1805 was the climax to the long-standing rivalry for command of the Atlantic between France and Britain. Though outnumbered, the British destroyed two-thirds of the enemy fleet and ended the French challenge to Britain's navy forever.

Trade and war

As European countries like Britain and France built up their overseas empires and their fleets of merchant ships, they also rivaled each other in the growth of their navies. The purpose of the new ships was to protect the new colonies and the merchant ships trading with them. If war broke out, warships either attacked the enemy's merchant vessels or cut off trade by blockading the enemy's ports.

The British and the French navies both almost doubled the number of their warships between 1720 and 1780. This showed how the growth in overseas trade had increased these navies' protection duties and the importance of the new colonies to the empire builders.

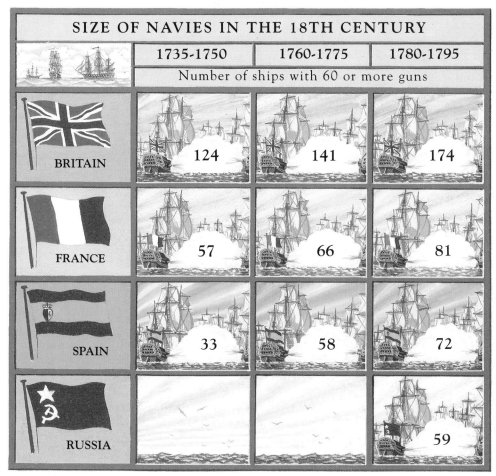

SIZE OF NAVIES IN THE 18TH CENTURY			
	1735-1750	1760-1775	1780-1795
	Number of ships with 60 or more guns		
BRITAIN	124	141	174
FRANCE	57	66	81
SPAIN	33	58	72
RUSSIA			59

Historians have a saying that "trade follows the flag." By 1800, five European countries had colonies overseas – Britain, France, Spain, Portugal and the Netherlands. Britain's empire was by far the largest, although most of it was uninhabited and unexplored. The European powers did not just want to own more land – empires were built for trade. The value of empires lay not so much in their size as in the goods that passed through their trading stations on the coasts. Overland traders brought their goods to the stations where they made deals with merchants from Europe.

Trading stations

Trading stations did not belong to the ruling government. They were owned and run by private groups of merchants like the British and the French East India companies. Some of these had their own private armies to keep order in the trading stations and protect them from attacks by local inhabitants. Many of the trading stations were fortified. For example, the trading station of the British East India Company in eastern India was called Fort William before it was renamed Calcutta. Sometimes the threat from outside the walls was real enough. Fort William was attacked and conquered in 1756 by the Indian ruler of Bengal.

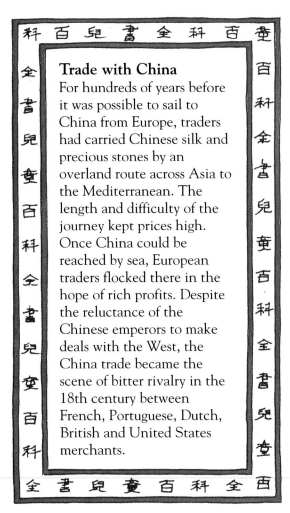

Trade with China

For hundreds of years before it was possible to sail to China from Europe, traders had carried Chinese silk and precious stones by an overland route across Asia to the Mediterranean. The length and difficulty of the journey kept prices high. Once China could be reached by sea, European traders flocked there in the hope of rich profits. Despite the reluctance of the Chinese emperors to make deals with the West, the China trade became the scene of bitter rivalry in the 18th century between French, Portuguese, Dutch, British and United States merchants.

Colonial trading stations collected raw materials for export that were brought overland from the surrounding area. They were also centers for the distribution of manufactured goods brought by the merchant ships of imperial countries.

Settlers and slaves

It was a short step from traders taking what the colonies produced naturally to settlers farming the land. Sailors and other visitors brought back tales of fertile and empty land ideal for crops such as cotton, sugar cane and tobacco, which could not be grown in Europe. The discoveries by European explorers of North and South America and the West Indies in the late 15th and 16th centuries were soon followed by British, French, Dutch, Spanish and Portuguese settlements. By about 1750, hundreds of ships were crossing the Atlantic each year to the East Coast ports of North America, the West Indies, and northeastern South America. France alone had 600 ships sailing to and from its West Indian colonies. Going westward they carried European manufactured goods such as iron tools and cloth. They brought back raw materials for use in European factories.

For settlers used to the uncertain climate of Europe, the ease of farming in more tropical regions seemed like a miracle. There was plenty of land. The climate was predictable. The crops were huge and healthy. The only problem was that large plantations in the West Indies and southern North America needed a large force of unskilled labor to work on the land. Where were these workers to come from? The answer lay in one of the most dreadful chapters in history – the development of the slave trade.

In the southern United States, black slaves were sold at auction as if they were cattle. Women with babies were particularly valuable, because the children – the slaves of the future – were sold with their mothers.

The slave trade

The British became the world leaders of the slave trade. Liverpool and Bristol were the European centers of the trade, together with the French port of Nantes. Over two million slaves had been taken from West Africa to the British colonies in the West Indies and North America by 1786. About 200 British ships took part in the trade.

They sailed from Europe to West Africa with cargoes of cloth, beads, mirrors and other cheap "trade goods." In Africa tribal chiefs were waiting with hundreds of captives, often their own people. Goods and human beings were exchanged, and the ships were packed with slaves chained side by side. The next leg of the voyage took the slaves across the Atlantic. Many people died on the way and were thrown overboard.

The slaves who survived were sold to plantation owners. In the 1750s a typical price was £40 (in 1994, $60). With their profits, the ships' masters bought sugar or tobacco as cargo for the third leg of the voyage. Starting out with cheap goods and returning with luxuries, the slave traders could not fail to make their fortunes.

Reformers such as William Wilberforce finally helped to banish slavery from history, as did the liberation of plantation slaves at the end of the American Civil War. The problem of cheap labor remained.

THE INDUSTRIAL REVOLUTION

A map of the world's shipping routes in 1800 would show how fast world trade had developed. Ships crisscrossed the Atlantic between Europe and the American continents. A steady stream of ships sailed from Europe down the west coast of Africa bound for India, the East Indies and occasionally China. The shores of Europe were alive with coastal shipping, but something was about to happen that would multiply world trade many times – the Industrial Revolution.

The start of industry

The Industrial Revolution is the name historians give to the changes in the way things were made in Europe and parts of the United States after about 1780. Slow, laborious and costly manual crafts carried on at home or in small workshops were replaced by faster, cheaper machine manufacture in factories. The first major industries to change were cotton spinning and weaving. Soon the Industrial Revolution spread to many other trades, such as printing, metalwork, furniture manufacture and toolmaking.

After about 1800, the energy to drive the factories' machines came from coal-fired steam engines. So the centers of European industry grew up close to coal-mining areas. In the U.S. these centers often developed near waterways that could power machines.

Looms in a cotton mill. They are driven by the belts connected to revolving shafts in the ceiling. The shafts were powered by a steam-engine.

Imports and exports

The Industrial Revolution stimulated world trade in two ways. First, the new factories were greedy for raw materials, many of which came from abroad. Second, overseas markets were needed for the factories' products. One example of this is what happened in the cotton industry. When cotton was spun and woven by hand it was a luxury. The new cotton mills could produce it so fast that in seven years the price per yard was slashed by two-thirds.

The demand for raw cotton made fortunes in the southern states of North America. It also provided work for the crews of hundreds of ships that brought the cotton crop to Europe and exported it again in the form of woven cloth.

The hand-loom weavers

The Industrial Revolution produced even greater changes in the wool industry. The spinning and weaving of woollen cloth in Europe went back hundreds of years. It was a "cottage" industry carried on in the homes of the spinners and weavers, using spinning wheels and looms operated by their hands or feet. Spinners bought the raw wool at market and weavers sold the cloth at fairs that were held regularly in the larger towns of the weaving areas.

When factories took over the wool industry, hand-spinners and weavers found themselves thrown out of work. They could go and work in the mills, if they lived close enough, but there was no longer any need for their skills. Just as today's computer revolution has put many people out of work, so the Industrial Revolution of 200 years ago forced people to forget their old skills and look for new jobs.

Power-looms put thousands of hand-loom weavers out of work, and their family businesses collapsed. Some weaving communities never recovered, such as Calton near Glasgow in Scotland.

Factory life

Working in the new factories of the Industrial Revolution introduced millions of people to something that had never seemed important before – time. To get the best return from their investment, factory owners kept their machines running as long as possible, from early morning to late at night. It was vital that the workforce should arrive on time at the start of the day, often as early as 5 A.M. Anyone who was late had to pay a fine that was taken off their pay at the end of the week.

Few factory workers had clocks in those days so they would pay a "knocker-up" to wake them in the mornings. The knocker-up had a long stick that he would rattle on the windows, waiting for an answer before he moved on. There would just be time for the workers to have something to eat and drink before the factory whistle sounded, warning them that they must be at their machines within a few minutes.

At the end of the long day, the factory whistle would sound again to signal that it was time to stop work. Six nights a week, there would be just time to have a meal before falling exhausted into bed, ready for the next morning.

The production of goods in larger quantities was only one aspect of the Industrial Revolution. Another was the introduction of new methods of distribution.

Steam powered the factories of the Industrial Revolution. It also brought about a revolution in transport. The first working railway opened in the north of England in 1825. Although the first train carried passengers, the railway's main purpose was to transport coal from the nearby mines to the port of Stockton. By making travel easier, railways were to bring important changes to people's lives. The money-making side of the railway industry, however, has always been freight, particularly the transport of bulk freight such as coal, metal ores, building materials and timber.

A world of railways

Railways spread quickly. There were only three short lengths of steam railway in the world in 1830, two in England and the third in the United States. By 1848, there were 6,250 miles (10,000 km) of railway line in Britain alone, and rail networks were spreading rapidly from Paris, Berlin and other European cities. By 1870, Europe's railways totaled 65,625 miles (105,000 km); in the United States there were 51,250 miles (82,000 km) of track, and railways were spreading across the world. They played an important part in opening up the interiors of North America and mainland Asia.

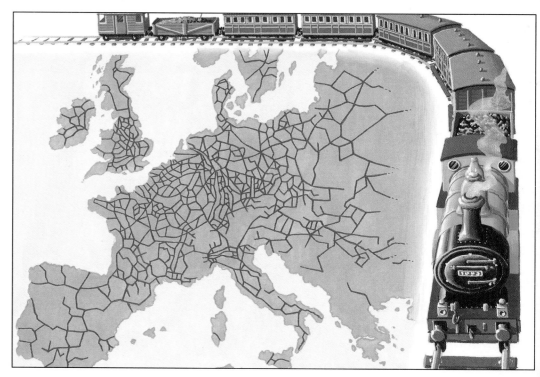

Locomotion, the steam locomotive built by George Stephenson for the opening of the Stockton and Darlington Railway in 1825.

Timing the trains

Time was vital to the running of the railways. This led to an important change in public timekeeping. Public clocks did not show a standard national time, even in a small country like Britain. For example, at Bristol, about 125 miles (200 km) west of London, local time was ten minutes behind London time. This caused obvious problems for travelers. In the early days of railways it also posed a safety hazard, because trains were separated along the track by a time interval. The answer was to introduce "railway time." In Britain this meant using London time. Train guards and railway policemen, the forerunners of signalmen, were supplied with accurate watches that they checked against each other whenever they could.

Accidents

Despite the careful checking of watches, running a railway on a time interval system was fraught with danger. There was no way for railway staff to communicate with each other before the electric telegraph was invented in the 1840s. Once a train had passed, a policeman might not know if it had broken down further along the line. When the proper time interval had passed, which might be only a few minutes on a busy line, he could send the next train on to certain disaster. This was the cause of many fatal accidents on the early railways as breakdowns were frequent.

Running on time

Both freight and passenger trains were planned to run on timetables, which was another reason for adopting a standard "railway time." Many passenger journeys involved connections between trains at junctions. A few minutes could make all the difference between a connection and a long wait for the next train.

The electric telegraph

Although the railways adopted it only slowly because of the cost, the electric telegraph revolutionized railway safety. It enabled stations and signal boxes to communicate by means of bells or the movements of a needle that gave coded messages. The telegraph could also be used to send time checks down the line.

The improvements in railway transportation encouraged ever more efficient factories.

Poor communication between railway employees could have terrible consequences.

One of Samuel Morse's earliest electric telegraphs, which transmitted and received messages in Morse code.

Suddenly it was important for everyone to know the time. There were trains to catch. People must not be late for work. It became essential to have a clock in the house. In Europe, clocks had been made expensively by hand, often by jewelers. In North America, carpenters had made clocks out of wood. There was a demand now for cheap clocks. The answer was to make them by machine out of identical parts, usually stamped out of brass. Today our homes are full of machines of various kinds. The first machine to become part of the furniture was the 19th-century, factory-made clock.

A clock and watchmaker's shop in about 1900. Most watches and clocks were made in factories by this time. Shops merely sold and repaired them.

Two examples of handmade lantern clocks from the 17th century. Both were made in London. Lantern clocks were designed to be hung on a wall.

The clock industry

Germany was the center of clockmaking in Europe, and so it was natural that German factories should be the first to produce cheap factory-made clocks. New England became the home of this developing industry in North America. In both countries, clocks were produced by the system called mass-production. Instead of painstakingly cutting and grinding the separate parts of each clock to fit together, large numbers of identical parts were stamped out by machines. They could then be fitted together by unskilled workers and mounted inside a case, which was also mass-produced. Chimes or bells were often added to make the clocks more attractive. In 19th-century homes, a clock was often displayed in the living room. This was usually an "eight-day" model that needed winding only once a week. In the bedroom upstairs, there would be a mass-produced alarm clock that could be set to ring in the morning to wake people up.

Sporting gun, with wheel-lock mechanism, 1623.

An early sewing machine.

The 19th century saw many articles formerly handmade in craft workshops produced in large numbers in factories. The rifle above was hand-built, but thousands were factory-made. Many small machines were easily assembled from interchangeable parts.

Burroughs, adding machine, 1897.

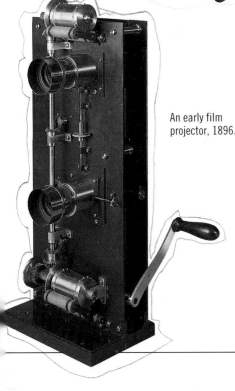

An early film projector, 1896.

Machines for everyone

It was not long before manufacturers realized that if clocks could be made quickly and cheaply by assembling machine-made parts, so could other kinds of small machines. Elias Howe was an American watchmaker who invented the first sewing machine for industry in 1845. This brought down the price of shop-bought clothes by eliminating hand-sewing. Another American called Isaac Singer saw how useful a sewing machine would be at home. He built up a business supplying mass-produced machines both for the clothing industry and for home use.

The idea of mass-production could be applied to any machine made up of metal parts. American and German inventors were not lacking in ideas. Some were merely fun objects such as musical boxes, but others were more practical. The inside or "frame" of a piano could be made by mass-production and, by the late 1800s, the piano had become part of the furniture of many homes – just like the clock.

Mass-produced machines are not confined to the home. Philo Remington was an American gunmaker who had used mass-production methods to supply frontiersmen with cheap weapons. He began to produce typewriters in 1874, which started an office revolution.

The rival powers

During the 19th century, the pattern of world power changed. It was based on trade as before, but new countries assumed control. Britain began the century as the undisputed leader in world trade, by having the biggest empire, the largest navy and the largest fleet of merchant ships. Not even France, the historical trading rival, could put up a real challenge to Britain's lead in the Industrial Revolution.

There was a change in mid-century. After recovering from the Civil War, the United States began to pull together as one nation and build up its industries. The separate states of Germany came together as one in 1871. New countries have new ideas, and the United States and Germany began steadily to increase their trade at the expense of Britain. They were looking ahead while Britain sat back, satisfied with its history. By 1900, Britain's role as the leader of world trade was ending.

In 1800 large areas of the world, such as the interiors of Africa and Australia, were unknown to the people outside them. Similarly large areas of scientific knowledge were still unexplored. For example, the ways in which disease spread were still a mystery to doctors and scientists. Little was known about energy or about the relationship between heat and light. The study of electricity was still at an early experimental stage and no practical use had been found for it. These and other scientific mysteries were solved during the 19th century.

An early example of precision toolmaking, this 1789 wheel-cutting machine was designed to cut the wheels of clock mechanisms.

The orrery (left) and the globe enabled scientists to understand and interpret natural phenomena.

Accurate timing

The making of accurate timekeepers aided science in two ways, one direct and the other indirect. Many experiments demanded careful timing, from observing the growth of disease organisms to measuring electrical currents. They also required precise measurement. The experience of clockmakers in precision engineering enabled them to produce a wide range of accurate measuring instruments for scientific work. German craftsmen became world leaders in this field, adapting their traditional skills in making clocks and watches.

Watching the stars

The 19th century saw a great surge of interest in astronomy, which led to the building of many of the world's great observatories. This was due to improvements in telescope technology and in glassmaking. The new glass used for lenses and mirrors produced images free from distortion. A network of government and university observatories was set up throughout Europe, North and South America, and Australasia. Precise timekeeping enabled them to pool their knowledge by comparing their observations.

The Lick Observatory on Mount Hamilton, California, was opened in 1887. At the time it contained the world's most powerful telescope.

Popular science

New scientific discoveries followed one another with exciting frequency in the 19th century. It seemed that there was no end to what science could do. Scientific ideas caught the imagination of people everywhere as lectures and demonstrations became popular forms of entertainment. People went eagerly to science museums where they could see scientific principles at work. The Smithsonian Institution in Washington, D.C., was founded in 1846, and was soon followed by many other countries. London's Science Museum opened in 1857. Most European countries had one or more museums of science by 1900.

People were also eager to read about science. In Britain they could obtain *Chambers' Journal*, while Americans read *Scientific American*, the French *La Nature* and the Dutch *De Natuur*. These magazines reported on scientific developments from around the world. They enabled readers to feel that they were taking an active part in the exciting discoveries that were being made.

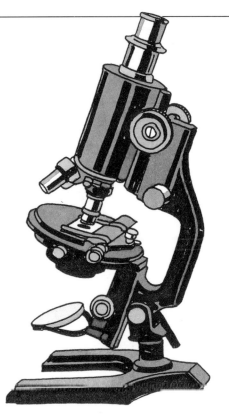

Preserving food

One important scientific discovery was an understanding of the organisms that cause decay in food. The pioneer in this field was the French biochemist Louis Pasteur. The aim of his first experiments was to stop wine from going sour. This could be done by heating the wine for a carefully timed period to a specific temperature. Later, the same idea was applied to milk and was called "pasteurization." This process was also used to preserve food in cans from about 1860, creating another new industry.

A painting, at the Royal Institution in London, of the laboratory in which the British scientist Michael Faraday carried out his experiments on electricity.

Time had become all-important by 1900 for most people in the industrialized world. They got up on time in order to be punctual at work. They often caught trains or streetcars to get there, which ran to timetables. In the evenings, they sometimes planned to arrive in time at a theater or a scientific lecture. Watches were not yet cheap enough for most people, but in towns and cities there was no difficulty in finding out the time. There were clocks which chimed out the hours on the outside of most churches, town halls and other public buildings.

Longer days

The invention of gaslight and, later, electric lamps meant that people could use their evenings at home for what they wanted to do, whether it was study or entertainment. Many families gathered around the piano for musical evenings, especially at weekends. Others played cards or other games. In the industrialized countries, children had to go to school, and public lending libraries opened in most towns and cities. Reading became a favorite pastime for millions of people. The day was no longer over when the sun set.

Workers spill through the factory gates after a day's labor.

Working hours

One of the results of the factory system was a change in the method of paying workers. At first they were paid a fixed amount of money for a day's work, as farm workers had been. Many factories soon began to work a shift system by splitting the day into two or even three parts. It became more convenient for employers and workers to agree on an hourly rate of pay. This system was helped by the invention of a machine that recorded the time that each worker started and stopped work. When workers arrived and left, they put a card into the machine, which stamped the time on it. There could then be no argument about the amount of time they had worked. This was called "punching in" and "punching out."

Spare time

Most people's working days became shorter during the 19th century. They had more time to themselves. It was a time of growth for the entertainment industry. A wide variety of entertainment was offered in large cities. There were boxing and wrestling matches, variety shows, serious theater, and concerts of all kinds of music. With more leisure time, people were able to watch sports on the weekend. Football and other spectator sports had previously been played by amateurs on any open space they could find. Professional sports were now introduced, played in stadiums built specially to hold large crowds.

Some people preferred to exercise themselves rather than watch other

people do it. Many joined cycling or hiking (country walking) clubs and enjoyed a day in the country on the weekend. These activities were very popular with young people who liked to get away from the noise and grime of the cities.

An actor in the Japanese kabuki theater. Kabuki plays were based on traditional stories and attracted packed audiences in Japan's cities.

Daylight saving

A problem arose when countries adapted a standard time. The sun does not keep clock time. Sunrise in summer occurs in the middle of the clock's "night." In 1907 a British builder called William Willett felt that time should be rearranged to suit people's convenience. His idea was that the clock should be moved forward by an hour in the summer to take advantage of the earlier daylight. His idea was adopted and spread to other countries after a great deal of argument. This is why clocks are put forward in the spring for daylight saving time and put back again in the autumn in many countries.

People were increasing their active life everywhere. The world was slowly becoming a smaller place.

In 1876, the Centennial Exhibition in Philadelphia celebrated the United States' scientific and industrial achievements in the 100 years since American independence from Britain.

The map of the world known to the people of Europe and North America when John Harrison made his chronometer included many large, empty spaces. The coasts of Africa, Australia and most of Asia were marked on it, but nothing was known about the interior of the continents. The people living in these continents knew nothing about the world outside.

Filling in the map

With the invention of accurate watches, explorers could chart their position on land or sea accurately to within a few miles. The 19th century saw the map of the world gradually filled in with detail. The explorers had many different motives for their dangerous and sometimes fatal expeditions. Some were missionaries. Others were looking for adventure. Still more were hoping to make their fortunes.

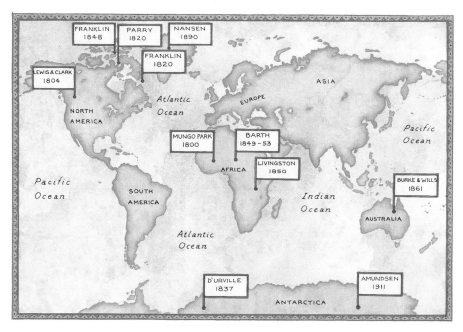

Opening up America

In 1803, Napoleon, First Consul of France, made the United States an amazing offer. He was ready to sell the huge area of southwestern North America owned by France for $12 million because he was desperate for money to pay for his wars in Europe. The U.S. president, Thomas Jefferson, accepted the offer at once. This led to one of exploration's greatest adventures.

The United States' new territory was almost unoccupied by settlers and most of it had not been explored by whites. Few settlers had ventured west of the Mississippi River. In May 1804, an expedition set out from St. Louis, on the Mississippi, to explore the new land and find a route over the Rocky Mountains to the Pacific. It was led by two army captains called Meriwether Lewis and William Clark. They took with them 45 men chosen for their pioneering experience.

At first they made good progress, but conditions soon got worse. The explorers were attacked by Sioux Indians. Winter was bitterly cold and the party had to build a fort to shelter in. They moved on over the Rockies when the spring came. Food became hard to find and they had to eat berries and crows. At last, they caught sight of the Pacific Ocean on November 7, 1805. The route to the west was open.

Exploration in the unknown interiors of the continents offered opportunities for adventurers and fortune-hunters.

Captain Scott's expedition party at
the South Pole in January 1912.

Into space

The idea of exploring space has been around for centuries, but it was not until the 1960s that humankind had the technology to break out of Earth's gravitational pull. Space exploration became possible through a combination of rocket technology, the development of metals that could withstand fierce heat, and the precise calculations and timekeeping that could be made by computers.

In the 1960s, the United States and the USSR took part in a "space race." The real aim was to show off their world power. The USSR was the first to send a man into space, in 1961, when Yuri Gagarin made one orbit of Earth before returning. Both countries landed unmanned spacecraft on the Moon, but it was an American, Neil Armstrong, who became the first human being to step on to the Moon's surface in July 1969. That has been the limit of human exploration so far, but unmanned craft have visited the nearer planets.

Such amazing journeys would not have been possible without great advances being made in communications technology.

Conquering the Poles

The Arctic Circle had been explored by Europeans searching for a route from the Atlantic to the Pacific. Sailors had also sighted Antarctica. But, by 1870, the two Poles remained the only unexplored areas in the world.

Many attempts to reach the North Pole in the 1890s failed. After many expeditions, a U.S. naval engineer called Robert Peary succeeded in April 1909.

The race to the South Pole was between Norway's Roald Amundsen and Britain's Captain Robert Scott. Unknown to Scott, Amundsen reached the Pole in December 1911. Scott arrived a month later. On the return journey, all the explorers in Scott's party died.

In 1971, U.S. astronauts on the *Apollo 15* mission made the fourth Moon landing. Here, James Irwin is standing beside his Lunar Roving Vehicle, saluting the American flag.

An important ceremony took place at Promontory Point near Salt Lake City, Utah on May 10, 1869. It was held at the place where two railway lines met. One line stretched eastward to Omaha, Nebraska, where it connected with other lines to the East Coast. To the west, the rails climbed over the Rockies to the Pacific. After five years' work, the two lines finally met when the last spike was driven home. For the first time, people could travel right across North America by rail. The United States had truly become one nation after the bruising Civil War. But there was a problem as soon as the trains began to run. It is nearly 2,500 miles (4,000 km) across North America from the Atlantic to the Pacific. Separate railway companies had their own local time, causing great confusion to long-distance travelers.

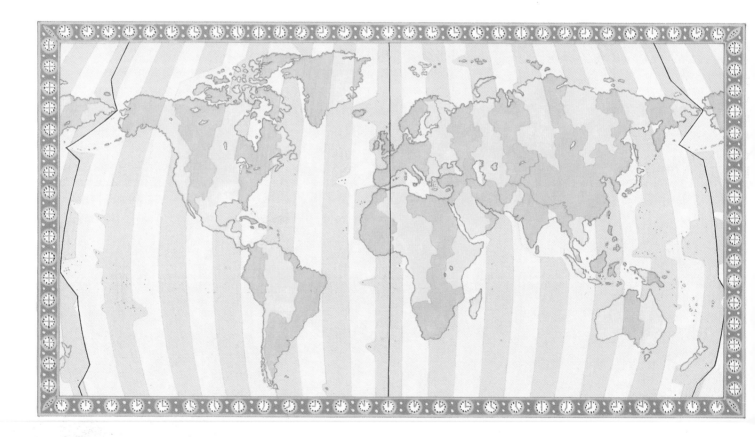

The 24 time zones, each 15 degrees of longitude wide, into which Earth is divided by international agreement.

The man with the answer

Sandford Fleming was a Scot who immigrated to Canada when he was 18 years old. In 1878, he devised the system of dividing the world into 24 "time zones" whose borders defined the time that would be kept. He later supervised the building of Canada's first transcontinental railway, opened in 1885.

A world divided by time

Time zones were adopted, not only by the American and Canadian governments and railway systems, but also by the whole world. Each zone is 15 degrees of longitude apart, with the Greenwich meridian as the starting-point. The time goes back by one hour for each zone to the west of Greenwich, and for each zone to the east it advances. The time in each zone is called "standard time." In North America there are five zones.

The division of the world into time zones raised another problem. Imagine that you are in an aircraft flying east around the world. Somewhere on the journey you will meet tomorrow's sunrise although for you and the other passengers on the plane, it will still be today! Endless confusion would result unless everyone could agree on when tomorrow becomes today and today becomes yesterday. The solution to this problem was to add to the time zone system an imaginary line on the map called the International Date Line. Travelers going west across the line change "today" to "tomorrow." Going east, they change "today" to 'yesterday."

A display in the Stock Exchange building in Jakarta, Indonesia, shows the time in various key cities around the world.

The most convenient place for the International Date Line was at 180 degrees longitude, which falls in the middle of the Pacific Ocean and crosses no land except at the poles. But the Line does not follow the 180 degrees meridian exactly all the way. There are two diversions. One was made so that Alaska and the Aleutian Islands have the same date as North America, and the other gives some South Sea Islands the same date as Australia and New Zealand.

The International Date Line and the time zones were accepted by an international conference held in Washington, D.C., in 1884.

Amsterdam   London   New York   Jakarta   Hong Kong   Tokyo   Kuala Lumpur

The fastest way to travel on land in 1800 was on horseback. Travel at sea depended on the winds. By 1900, rail networks covered all industrialized countries and were spreading in the undeveloped world, while steamships carried most of the world's trade. People could move about faster and more easily than at any time in history.

Ideas on the move

It was not only people that were on the move. Ideas could travel fast as well. Most countries had set up postal systems by about 1880. Once a luxury, sending a letter had become a service that anyone could afford. The mail also became an important tool of business. An international agreement signed in 1875 made the mail a worldwide system.

Another result of improved communications was a boom in the sale of newspapers and magazines. Mail and newspaper distribution became even faster when airmail was introduced within Europe and the United States in 1919, and later between continents.

The first regular airmail service in the United States was set up in 1919, when daily flights carried letters between New York City and Cleveland, Ohio.

A modern telephone exchange in Rochester, New York. It controls the switching of international calls.

Together with fax and other telecommunications signals, telephone calls are beamed from one country to another via satellite dishes.

The telecommunications revolution

The discovery of electricity was quickly followed by a stream of inventions that we now call telecommunications. The first of these was the electric telegraph, invented by Samuel Morse in the United States. By 1865, telegraph wires straddled the United States and Europe, and the two continents were linked by a cable under the Atlantic. One of the main uses of the international telegraph was to transmit news around the world. Also in the United States, Alexander Graham Bell demonstrated the first telephone in 1876. Within a few years it had become essential for business and personal use at home, for those who could afford it. Meanwhile, an Italian named Guglielmo Marconi was experimenting with radio telegraphy. He broadcast his first message in 1897 and had sent a message across the Atlantic by 1901. There was steady progress from then on, to today's worldwide radio and television services.

Electronic navigation

Radio is the basis of modern navigation at sea, in the air and in space. Aircraft flights are made along "airways" made up of radio signals that are received on the flight deck and keep the aircraft on course. The takeoff and landing of aircraft are also controlled by radio signals. These precautions are vital because of the fast speeds of aircraft and the number of them in the sky over busy areas.

Radar is an electronic navigational aid that uses radio waves. These are bounced off objects in their path, and the objects show up on a display. Almost all airplanes and ships carry radar.

It is difficult to imagine anyone living today without an awareness of time. It controls our activities at work and at leisure. We have become slaves to the clock in many ways. Most people take vacations so that they can live in such a way that time does not matter for a week or two.

A hard day's work

Factories are places where time matters. Manufacturers want to use their machinery and workers efficiently. They also need to know exactly how much it costs to make their products. One of the ways of achieving these aims is called "time and motion study." It involves studying the different operations that are needed to make a product and seeing if they can be speeded up, or even cut out altogether.

Time and motion study techniques were first developed in 1880 by an American manager named Frederick Taylor. Although much altered, his ideas are still used in factories today.

This vacuum cleaner of 1910 was heavy and cumbersome compared with the machines available today.

Time and motion study is a method of achieving maximum efficiency and productivity in manufacturing.

Saving time

As people became more aware of time, they began to think about "saving" it. Much time and effort was spent in the home on boring and repetitive jobs such as lighting fires, cleaning, polishing, and washing clothes. New York, London and Vienna had public electricity supplies by the 1880s. Once homes had electricity, a host of "time-saving" machines came into use. The first electric vacuum cleaner appeared in 1901. By 1928, well over a million cleaners were sold every year in the United States alone. Electric washing machines were on the market by 1914. Spin driers followed in 1920.

Time control

Switches give instant control over electricity. A switch combined with a clock enables electrical devices to be turned on and off automatically. One of the first uses of time switches was to turn electric street lights on at dusk and off at dawn. Time switches are used for many purposes today. In our homes, they switch ovens and lamps on and off and enable us to program video recorders to record television programs days or even weeks ahead. In banks and offices, time switches are used to prevent safes being opened by intruders in the night.

Timekeeping is a critical element in engineering research work. Here, a scientist is using a spectroscope to study the composition of gases.

Computer time

An electronic clock in the form of a silicon chip is at the heart of every computer. It is part of the computer's central processing unit. The computer could not operate without the clock. Computer programs carry out operations step by step at high speed. When a computer is in use, thousands of electrical signals travel around its electrical circuits every second. The clock transmits a regular electronic beat rather like the beat of a metronome but much faster. The beat controls the flow of the signals so that they do not get out of order.

The stress of time

One of the disadvantages of living in a society where the clock is all-important is that people tend to have competing calls on their time. For example, we want to spend time playing with our friends, but we also have to study. We want to see the late movie on television, but we have to be up early in the morning for school. Many people suffer from stress because of these clashes of interest. This is why it is important for everyone to have "time for themselves."

One area of life where time creates stress problems is that of air travel.

One of the most important changes of the 20th century has been the growth in air travel, for both business and pleasure. Only 50 years ago, most people who went abroad traveled by sea. Long-distance railways carried passengers across the continents. Today, air travel is an everyday experience for many people. Ocean liners no longer cruise on regular services across the oceans, and many long-distance railways carry only heavy freight such as timber or coal. The other side of the world was many weeks away before the age of flight. It can now be reached in a few hours.

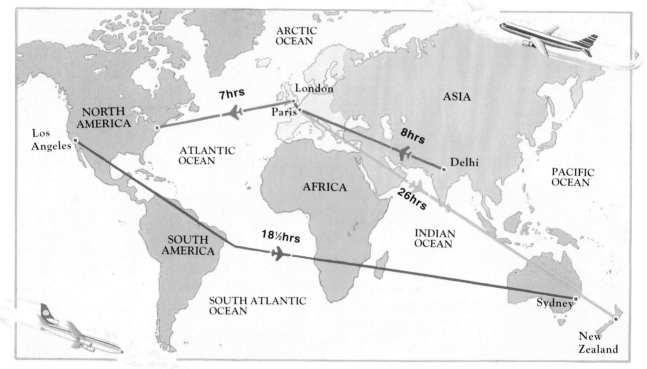

These flight times between the four corners of the world would have seemed incredible only 50 years ago. Nowadays, they are part of everyday experience.

Safety in the air

The world's busiest airports include those in Chicago and Dallas-Fort Worth in the United States, and London's Heathrow in England. They handle hundreds of aircraft arrivals and departures each day. The airways that link major airports are crowded with aircraft. Air safety depends on separating flights by both time and distance.

The pilot is given a flight plan before every flight. This tells him or her the height and speed at which to fly, and the estimated time of arrival (ETA) at the destination. Air traffic controllers slot the flight into all the others along the same route, separating them by time and height. Computer controls ensure that the flight plan is followed.

Aircraft take off and land under the orders of airport control. If a number of aircraft are waiting to land, they join a "stack." This is an oval course that aircraft fly one above the other. They join it at the top and gradually move down until it is their turn to land. Once again, time and distance are the key to safety.

Business and pleasure

In 1935, the world's airlines carried fewer than five million passengers. Today, they carry a billion passengers a year and make about 40,000 flights each day.

The growth in air travel has changed the world in many different ways. Most air travel is done by business people so that now international business is often carried on "face to face" instead of by letter or telephone. World leaders travel frequently to meet each other to try to solve international problems. Entertainers, writers, musicians, artists and sports personalities are able to travel the world and build up international reputations. However, the biggest change for most people is the ease of going abroad on vacation and experiencing the food, arts and lifestyle of other cultures. Tourism boosted by air travel has brought new wealth to parts of the world such as the southeast coast of Spain, Florida and the Seychelles.

The Boeing 747 "jumbo" jet is the world's leading passenger carrier. It was introduced in 1970.

The body clock

People who travel frequently by air often suffer from a condition called "jet lag." They may find it hard to sleep, or to stay awake, and may suffer from stomach upsets. The reason is that the systems that control their daily lives, their "body clocks," cannot cope with rapid changes. For example, someone flying from the United States to Japan passes through at least six time zones. If they have breakfast before they leave, they arrive in time to have another one! Then there is another whole day ahead before bedtime. The human body can cope with this now and then, but if it is repeated it can lead to stress and other health problems.

Air travel is one of the quicker ways that people can move from place to place. Humans have pushed the boundaries of speed and time throughout history. Can time continue to be speeded up?

People have always believed that speed was dangerous to health. One English "expert" in the 1830s, Dr. Dionysius Lardner, claimed that traveling by train at 37½ miles per hour (60 kmph) would shake the brain to pieces. He urged Queen Victoria not to be so reckless as to take a train journey. But she did so, in 1842, and afterward became a keen railway traveler. Since then, supersonic flight and space flight have shown that the human body can withstand huge speeds, with the protection of pressurized cabins. As space flight continues, the frontiers of speed are still being pushed back.

			Speed Comparisons
First cars		5 mph/ 8 kph	
Wright's first powered flight		7 mph/ 25 kph	
Stagecoach		10 mph/ 16 kph	
Stockton-Darlington railway 1825		20 mph/ 32 kph	
Japanese 'Bullet train'		130 mph/ 210 kph	
Experimental car, 1970s		180 mph/ 290 kph	
French TGV train		188 mph/ 300 kph	
Concorde		1305 mph/ 2100 kph	
Sputnik 1		18000 mph/ 28000 kph	

Before the introduction of railways, road services between major cities were provided by stagecoaches.

Human achievement

Even without the help of machinery human beings have steadily improved their own performance under the stimulus of competition. Athletics have become a popular pastime in the 20th century, spurred on by the revival in 1896 of the Olympic Games. These games are held once every four years in a different country and provide a showcase for human achievement.

A British runner named Roger Bannister became the first man to run a mile (1.609 kilometers) in under four minutes in 1954. World speed records over various distances have tumbled since then. Modern timekeeping can record performance to within a hundredth of a second.

The start of a major cycling race. Like athletics, cycling is a sport in which accurate timekeeping has encouraged the setting of new standards.

Relativity

An unknown German scientist named Albert Einstein published some research in 1905 that was to change the scientific view of speed and time. Until then, scientists had believed that space, time and speed were absolute; in other words, that they had a fixed value. Einstein proved that this is not always true. He showed that space and time were linked, but not always in the same way. At speeds approaching the speed of light, almost 186,000 miles per second (300,000 km sec), time seems to pass more slowly. As time passes more slowly, objects traveling at such high speeds seem to last longer. Einstein also showed that the force of gravity has an effect on time, and that speeds close to the speed of light can change the shape and nature of matter.

Albert Einstein called his ideas the special theory and the general theory of relativity. They led to the development of nuclear physics, among other things.

The universe is made up of millions of bodies moving at great speeds in space. Einstein's ideas raised new questions about what the universe is like, how it began – and how, one day, it will end.

Bang and crunch

Einstein's ideas led to the development of the "big bang" theory as the explanation of how the universe began. According to this theory, all the matter in the universe was gathered together until a tremendous explosion blew it apart, forming the galaxies. The galaxies are still moving apart. Some scientists believe that one day, in many billions of years' time, they will stop moving apart, come together again, and the universe will end in a "big crunch."

almanac An annual publication showing the position of heavenly bodies on each day and night of the year, issued to help with navigation.

astrolabe An instrument for measuring the altitudes, positions and movements of heavenly bodies. It has a movable pointer pivoted at the center of a disc marked in degrees.

big bang theory The idea that the separate parts of the universe were formed billions of years ago by the explosion of a densely packed mass of matter.

body clock The system within the nerve cells of the body that determines when an animal feels hungry, sleepy or wakeful.

chronometer An accurate mechanical clock that is designed to withstand the motion of a ship at sea and changes in temperature.

compass An instrument containing a magnetized pointer or "needle" that shows the direction of magnetic north. From this, the other compass points can be measured.

daylight saving time The adjustment of clocks and watches during the summer months so that the hours of daylight begin and end earlier.

dead reckoning A system of navigation by measuring the distance traveled along a predetermined course within a period of time.

exports Goods sent from one country to another.

gravity The Earth's gravitational pull is the force that attracts objects toward Earth and keeps them there unless a greater force, such as rocket propulsion, overcomes it.

imports Goods brought into one country from another.

Industrial Revolution The change that began in the 18th century from handmade to machine-made goods, using steam power.

International Date Line An imaginary line passing through the Pacific Ocean. Travelers crossing it from east to west add a day to the calendar, and those crossing from west to east subtract a day.

jet lag Confusion and tiredness caused by frequent interruptions of natural sleep rhythms as a result of fast air travel.

latitude The distance from the Equator of an object on Earth's surface, measured by imaginary lines on the surface about 69 miles (110 kilometers) apart.

local time The time at points on the Earth's surface which are on the same meridian or line of longitude.

longitude The distance along the Equator, measured up to 180 degrees east or west of the prime meridian, which is 0 degrees.

mainspring The coiled spring that provides the driving force for a mechanical clock or watch.

mass production The manufacture of machinery from stocks of interchangeable parts which are put together on an assembly line.

mechanical A mechanical clock or watch is one driven by a clockwork motor rather than by electricity.

meridian Line of longitude. The prime meridian passes from the North Pole to the South Pole through Greenwich in London, England.

metronome A pointer operated by a clockwork motor that beats time regularly, used in training musicians.

pasteurization A process for sterilizing milk by heating it for a timed period, followed by rapid cooling. It was invented by the French chemist Louis Pasteur.

pendulum A metal or wooden rod pivoted to a mechanism at one end and with a weight at the other.

punching in/punching out A system of registering the time at which an employee arrives at and leaves work by stamping the time on a personal card.

railway time Standard time kept by all the employees of a railway to ensure that timetables are accurate throughout the network.

sextant An optical instrument for measuring the angle of the sun from Earth's surface, which enables the observer's latitude to be calculated.

shift system A system of working in which one group of employees works for part of the day and another group for another part. The hours worked are called a shift.

speed The distance traveled by a moving object in any direction within a certain period of time. The speed of a moving object in a particular direction is called velocity.

standard time 1. A setting of time that is used as a reference in calculating longitude by comparing it with local time.
2. The time observed with a time zone.

switch A device that enables electricity to be turned on and off. A time switch is linked to a clock that operates it automatically.

supersonic At a speed greater than the speed of sound.

telecommunications Communication over a distance using electricity, for example the telephone, radio or television.

telegraph A method of communicating along wires using codes made up of bursts of electricity.

time and motion study A method of improving factory production by studying the time taken by employees, and the movements they have to make, to carry out tasks.

time zones Areas of the world, 15 degrees of longitude wide, based on the prime meridian. For each zone west of the Prime Meridian, time goes back by one hour and for each zone east it advances by one hour.

theories of relativity Two theories developed by the scientist Albert Einstein. He suggested that when objects approach the speed of light time seems to pass more slowly, and also that at those speeds objects can change their shape and structure.

INDEX

Further Reading

HISTORY OF THE AMERICAN CLOCK BUSINESS – Jerome. (Bristol, CT: American Clock & Watch Museum, Inc., 1991).

Kalman, Bobbie. TOOLS AND GADGETS (New York: Crabtree Publishing Company, 1992).

Spangenburg, Ray and Kit Moser. THE HISTORY OF SCIENCE IN THE EIGHTEENTH CENTURY (New York: Facts On File, 1993).

——————— . THE HISTORY OF SCIENCE IN THE NINETEENTH CENTURY (New York: Facts On File, 1993).

——————— . THE HISTORY OF SCIENCE FROM 1895–1945 (New York: Facts On File, 1994).

Willard, John W. SIMON WILLARD AND HIS CLOCKS (New York: Dover Publications, Inc., 1968).